Story by Sergei Prokofiev

PETER
and the WOLF

Retold and illustrated by

MICHÈLE LEMIEUX

HARCOURT BRACE & COMPANY

Orlando Atlanta Austin Boston San Francisco Chicago Dallas New York
Toronto London

The Russian composer Sergei Prokofiev wrote the musical tale *Peter and the Wolf* to introduce children to the orchestra. Each character in the story is represented by an instrument: the bird by a flute, the duck by an oboe, the cat by a clarinet, the grandfather by a bassoon, the wolf by a French horn, Peter by a violin, and the hunters by the kettle and bass drums. Now here is our story:

Once upon a time there was a boy named Peter. He lived with his grandfather in a house surrounded by a high wall. Outside the wall lay a meadow with a pond and a tall tree. Beyond the meadow was a deep, dark forest.

Early one morning Peter opened the gate and went out into the big, green meadow.

On a branch of the tall tree sat Peter's friend, a little bird. He chirped happily, "All is quiet. All is quiet." All *was* quiet. Not even a breeze rippled the water of the pond.

Soon a duck came waddling by. Glad to see that Peter hadn't shut the gate, she had decided to take a swim in the deep pond. Seeing the duck, the little bird flew down beside her in the grass for a closer look: "What kind of bird are you if you can't fly?"

"What kind of bird are you," the duck replied, "if you can't swim?" And she dived into the pond.

They argued and argued, the duck swimming around in the pond, the little bird hopping along the bank.

Suddenly something caught Peter's attention—it was a cat, creeping through the high grass.

"While the bird is busy arguing," the cat was thinking, "I'll just grab him!"

"Look out!" cried Peter. The bird flew straight up into the tree while the duck quacked angrily at the cat . . . from the middle of the pond.

The cat paced round and round the tall tree, thinking, "Is it worth climbing up so high? By the time I get there, the bird will have flown away!"

Just then Peter's grandfather came out of the gate. He was very angry. "The meadow is a dangerous place," his grandfather scolded. "Suppose a wolf came out of the forest. What then?"

Peter paid no attention. He wasn't afraid of wolves. Nevertheless, Grandfather took Peter firmly by the hand, led him home, and locked the gate.

No sooner had Peter gone than a big gray wolf *did* come out of the forest.

In a flash, the cat scrambled up the tree.
The duck quacked louder and louder
and, in her panic, jumped right out of the
pond. But no matter how fast she tried
to run, she couldn't escape the wolf. He
was getting closer and closer, nearer
and nearer, catching up with her, and
then…he got her! And, in one gulp, he
swallowed her.

And now this is how things stood:

The cat was sitting on one branch of the tree. The bird was sitting on another . . . not too close to the cat. And the wolf, still hungry, was walking round and round the tree, looking up at them both with greedy eyes.

Peter stood behind the gate watching all that was going on. Without the slightest fear he ran into the house, found a strong rope, and climbed with it to the top of the high wall. One of the branches of the tree stretched out over the wall. Grabbing hold of this branch, Peter easily pulled himself into the tree.

"Listen," he whispered to the bird. "Fly down and circle around the wolf's head. But be careful he doesn't catch you."

The little bird flew so close that he almost brushed the wolf's nose with his wings. The wolf snapped angrily at him from this side and that. Oh, how the bird teased the wolf! And how the wolf tried to catch him! But the bird was far too clever.

Meanwhile Peter tied one end of the rope tightly around the branch. He then made a lasso out of the other end and, lowering it carefully, caught the wolf by the tail and pulled with all his might.

Feeling himself caught, the wolf began to
jump wildly about trying to free himself.

But his jumping only pulled the rope
tighter and tighter around his tail.

Just then three hunters came out of the woods. They were following the wolf's trail and shooting as they went. *Boom! Boom!*

From high up in the tree Peter shouted,
"Don't shoot!

"The bird and I have already caught the wolf.
You can help us take him to the zoo!"

So they all set off in a triumphant procession. First came Peter; behind him came the hunters, leading the wolf; last came the cat and Peter's grandfather, who shook his head and grumbled, "All well and good. But if Peter *hadn't* caught the wolf? What then?"

Above them all flew the little bird, chirping merrily, "Look how brave we are, Peter and I. Look what we've caught!"

And if you listen very carefully, you will hear the duck quacking—very softly, of course—inside the wolf. For the wolf, in his haste, had swallowed the duck whole!

To Wolfgang

Oil paints were used for the full-color artwork.
The text type is 16 point Congress Regular.

This edition is published by special arrangement with Morrow Junior Books, a division of William Morrow & Company, Inc.

Grateful acknowledgment is made to Morrow Junior Books, a division of William Morrow & Company, Inc. for permission to reprint *Peter and the Wolf*, retold and illustrated by Michèle Lemieux. Copyright © 1991 by Michèle Lemieux.

Printed in the United States of America

ISBN 0-15-302170-5

4 5 6 7 8 9 10   035   97 96 95